IF

BRIDGET CORDIS

authorHOUSE®

AuthorHouse™
1663 Liberty Drive
Bloomington, IN 47403
www.authorhouse.com
Phone: 1-800-839-8640

Published by AuthorHouse 11/15/2012

ISBN: 978-1-4772-7971-7 (sc)
ISBN: 978-1-4772-7972-4 (e)

Library of Congress Control Number: 2012919182

To my late mother, Joyce Babb, who also sought to let us
know that there is a God above who is looking over us.

To my Bible School Teacher, Doctor Mortimer Inniss,
who used the scriptures at all times to let us understand,
that without Holiness we all would be lost, even if we were
in the church every time the doors were opened.

To my husband, Jason and sister, Grace, who encouraged
me to pursue the task of writing this book.

To all of my spiritual sisters and brothers, especially sister Beatrice,
who prayed with me often as I started and stopped writing this book.

To my Pastor, Cecil Henry, who encouraged me and others, to do
what is necessary to fulfill our responsibility to God and man.

To my Lord Jesus Christ and the sweet Holy Spirit, who
have kept me and helped me to complete this task.

Table of Contents

Preface

There is a spirit of deception that visits every Christian. It manifests itself in varying forms in our lives. However, regardless of its manifestation, its main purpose is to keep us, the Redeemed of the Lord, in a sinful state so that we would not be able to participate in the Rapture.

Its primary deception is that we are humans and we must sin, which the Webster Dictionary defines as 'a willful violation of some religious or moral principle'. Sometimes we believe that deception and do not even try to live upright in the sight of God. Sometimes the deceiver, the devil, makes us feel that we are justified in our behavior so there is no need to repent or change, if we are mean and unforgiving to others, letting us believe that if we forgive someone we make them get away with whatever they did. Another deception is that we are better than others. When the spirit of pride rises up in us we enjoy that feeling of superiority and our behavior can be very obnoxious. Another deception, which can keep us sinning without any desire to stop, is once saved always saved. The final deception I will mention is that we have an advocate with the Father and he will intercede on our behalf.

I was once fully taken in with these deceptions, and believed all the lies the enemy of my Soul poured out, until I attended the Bible Center of Brooklyn, INC. School of Evangelism, and one of my teachers, the President, Dr. Mortimer Inniss, painstakingly used the scriptures and opened my darkened understanding to the deception of the devil. Using the scriptures he showed us that *we can and must live* in this sinful world and not commit sin. He helped us to understand that God, who said in *Leviticus, 11:45 "For I am the Lord that bringeth you up out of the Land of Egypt, to be your God: ye shall therefore be holy, for I am holy,"* would never ask anyone to do anything that was not possible.

After that enlightenment I thanked God that my *end* did not come while I was under the deception of the enemy of our Souls, in a sinful state. I pray that as you read this book, a spirit of discernment would be granted unto you and you would be able to discern the subtle presence of Satan, and with the help of the Holy Spirit, resist him so that he would flee from you.

Introduction

The life of a Believer is a challenging one. We go from high points to low points. We are at a high point when we first enjoy salvation, knowing that we have been saved, despite the fact that our sins were as scarlet and they have become white as snow. We are excited that those sinful things, which we did, have been cast into the sea of forgetfulness, never to be remembered anymore by our forgiving God. We are happy that God's grace and mercy watched over us while we were out there doing things, which were not pleasing in the sight of God; things that would have certainly sealed our fate in hell if our *end* had come with us in that state.

Then we have our lows. We have our spiritual tests and we fail. We are embarrassed. We wonder why God allowed us to do such a thing after He knows we gave Him our hearts. We even start questioning if indeed we were saved.

During our Christian journey we sometimes face challenges we never faced before; sickness or death in the family, financial challenges, strife in the workplace or strife with friends, and the list goes on. We are afraid to share our concerns/problems because we feel we would be judged (like Job was by his friends), as not living right with God. We struggle with varying emotions until by the grace of God we hear a life saving message and with the help of the Holy Spirit we get back on track, stronger in our faith in God.

Sometime we become so proud of how we are doing that we forget where we came from and the challenges we faced. As a result we demonstrate contempt for individuals who have not yet come to Jesus and are wallowing in sin. We sometimes show disdain for those have come and are struggling with their walk with God. Sometimes we hear of the shortcoming of individuals and we chastise them so badly that they separate themselves from the body of Christ, and even from God eventually, just as Adam and Eve did when they disobeyed God. Lest we put our Souls in a balance let us reflect on *Galatians 6:1 "Brethren, if a man is overtaken in a fault, ye which are spiritual, restore such a one in the spirit of meekness; considering thyself, lest thou also be tempted."*

Sometimes we find that we verbalize loudly about the sins of others, while we ourselves are consciously or unconsciously committing the same or some other sins. Homosexuality, a very serious sin, is denounced very often from the pulpit, rightly so. However occurrences have shown that some of those who denounced these acts were allegedly involved in them themselves. A very famous pastor, who was a prominent anti-gay activist, was exposed when a male prostitute recognized him on television and revealed his alleged secret sinful lifestyle. Another such pastor was exposed, when young men in his church accused him of alleged homosexual activity with them and lavishing them with gifts. It was reported that the pastor, who was being sued by the young men settled the matter out of court. A pastor, on his television program, stated how while he was in the pulpit giving sermons he was injecting himself with drugs through a needle in his toe. He praised his guest pastor on the program, whom he said had visited his church, and whom God had used to deliver a message, which freed him from the shackles of drugs, which was contaminating God's temple, his body.

Preachers, whether we preach regularly or occasionally, have been known to commit all sorts of sins, and unless caught, or delivered by the Holy Spirit we remain in a gall of bitterness. Those of us, who preach the word of God, must bear in mind what Paul states in *1 Corinthians 9:27 "But I keep under my body, and bring it into subjection: lest that by any means, when I have preached to others, I myself should be a cast away."*

I have emphasized some of the issues preachers face, because, the congregation feels that preachers have it all together and do not normally pray for them to be delivered from sin. It is necessary for the congregation to remember that their preachers are humans, with the same sinful nature, and need to be covered with prayers against the wiles of the devil.

May God grant us success over the devil as we prepare for Eternity.

If

If the *end* of our existence on earth were to come now, where would we spend Eternity? This is a general question to each and every one of us. Though the question comes to all of us, it is a question we would have to decide upon individually.

This question is addressed to the one who says there is no God; to the one who says there is a God, but does not care to be bothered now; to the one who says I can serve God in any form or manner, as well as to the one who says there is a God and seeks to acquaint himself with that God, and live a life pleasing in the sight of that God.

What is the *end* of existence I am speaking about? The *end* is that period of time when an individual, in this human form ceases to exist upon the earth. Events (deaths) have shown that man was not made to inhabit this earth for an indefinite period of time. We often recognize/celebrate individuals who live to one hundred years and more. Never-the-less they eventually die. Scientists are diligently exploring all possibilities to see how they can extend longevity. Some individuals are prepared to spend lots of money to extend their lives and youthfulness. However age still moves on and when the time comes for us to die, we will die, or leave this earth... *Hebrews 9:27 states "It is appointed unto men once to die, but after this the judgment".* The Bible also states that some will leave this earth without tasting death. "*Then we which are alive and remain shall be caught up together with them in the clouds, to meet the Lord in the air: and so shall we ever be with the Lord."1 Thessalonians 4:17.* This experience, which many Believers excitedly anticipate, is known as 'The Rapture'

While it is often said that folks will be born, live, get old and then die, the reality of life has shown that many are dying even before they grow old. Hardly a day goes by without one hearing of a child, or youth who has died, whether tragically or from an incurable illness. It is therefore necessary for young and old, men and women to prepare ourselves to stand before our God on Judgment Day, because no one knows when one's time on earth will come to an *end*, because we can say as David *"My times are in thy hand." Psalm 31:15*. Only God knows when our *end* will come.

Some may wonder, 'why is this writer writing about such a morbid subject?' I am writing about reality. Whether we admit it or not almost everyone is preoccupied with living; that is to avoid dying. We try to eat right and exercise so that we can remain healthy. Some of us are almost prepared to give away all of our rights so that the government can keep us safe from the terrorist. Some spend much money on security systems in order to keep themselves safe, not knowing or forgetting that *"the horse is prepared against the day of battle: but safety is of the Lord." Proverbs 21:31*

Individuals spend a lot of money on all sorts of items that are promised to guarantee longevity; but the fact is that no one can prevent us from dying when the time comes. We hear of all sorts of tragedy, from the Titanic, the Psunami, earthquakes, mud slides, house fires, horrible vehicle accidents, plane crashes and other calamities. While many die, some walk away with little or no injuries. No human being can decide that another will die on a particular day, if that is not to be. Execution dates have been known to be set for some condemned to die and had to be postponed or cancelled altogether. We hear of individuals firing weapons with the aim of ending another's life and the weapons are mysteriously disabled from firing or the bullets miss the intended targets, even hitting and killing others, for whom the bullets were not intended. We read of persons being badly wounded and left to die, and live to tell the tale. We read of coal miners being buried under ground and one or two surviving, while the others perish. In 2010, 33 miners from Chile were buried underground for 60 plus days and all survived. When we look at the lives of those who perished and those who survived, there is nothing that we can say is special about any one.

I would like to say now, that death is the only thing, which levels the playing field for everyone on this earth, regardless of color, race, economic status, religious standing or any other distinguishing features.

Many persons can boast of several things, though their boasting may be short lived. The crash of the stock market can and has caused billionaires to become millionaires, and millionaires to lose that status. The greed of unscrupulous individuals can cause an individual, who was once very rich to become a pauper overnight. Bernard Madoff's Ponzi scheme did exactly that. Some, experiencing such a change in status, may become so heart- broken that they may end their lives, by committing suicide, as they could not face those, to whom they had boasted, without having something to boast about. The most prolific sportsman, can boast about his prowess today, and tomorrow lose the ability to do anything for himself/ herself, due to an injury. Disgraced from poor decision making can cause someone, who was once revered, to hang his or her head in shame. Some persons can boast of no earthly possession or talent. However we all can make this claim, without thought of contradiction *ONE DAY I WILL LEAVE THIS EARTH.* As such we all must be prepared for that *DAY.*

THE NEED FOR PREPARATION

One may ask why should we prepare for that *DAY* of which we all can lay claim? I would ask why shouldn't we? We prepare for the birth of a child while the pregnancy may be a pseudo pregnancy, (a false pregnancy which gives the female all the symptoms associated with a real pregnancy), just to learn that it is no pregnancy, and at the end of term and all the preparation there is no baby. What a disappointment. We prepare for graduation, when sometimes we may find that even our best efforts were not good enough, sometimes genuinely or sometimes due to discrimination. In some instances some people become discouraged and refuse to continue to study. Some prepare for a marriage, checking to the last minute to see that everything is in place. The invitees arrive and are in the church, the hall is prepared for the reception. The lavish banquet is spread. Everyone is anxiously waiting to see how the groom looks, and how his eyes will twinkle when his bride arrives. Suddenly there is an announcement. The invitees listen and then gasp in astonishment, as they hear 'there will be no wedding one of the parties has changed his or her mind'. What a disappointment.

This writer once prepared to accept an award on behalf of the military organization, with which she once worked. My military boots were at its highest standard ever. My uniform was immaculate and I was well turned out. I encouraged myself not to be nervous, as I rehearsed in my mind all I had to do as I went to receive the award. I waited, and waited, and waited for the driver to pick me up. When the time had passed and I knew I could not be picked up anymore, I disappointedly took off my clothes. The driver had forgotten to pick me up. I was extremely disappointed and welcomed the loving, comforting words of my family. You can certainly imagine the disappointment of the jilted partner. With all that can happen, which is beyond our control mankind still prepares for a whole host of events. So why should we not prepare for leaving this earth, when it is a certainty that one day we will leave this earth.

In this material world in which we live we may appear before a judge with a superb lawyer, especially if the charge is a very serious one. The defense team may juggle the facts, look for the weaknesses in the prosecutor's case and win the defendant an acquittal. After the acquittal the fame of that lawyer may sky rocket. Some individuals capitalize on such a system and continue to be perpetrators of crime. However the *Judge*, before whom we will all stand when we leave this earth, is all seeing and all knowing. There will be no chance to juggle the facts and there will be no use of any smart lawyer as we all will stand individually before that *Judge*. Everyone will have to give an account of his/her stewardship on earth when the *end* comes. *Revelation 20:12 states And I saw the dead, small and great, stand before God, and the books were opened: and another book was opened, which is the Book of life: and the dead were judged out of those things which were written in the books, according to their works."*

The *end* can come at a time when we least expect. Even as I am writing this book the *end* can come before I am finished with it or before I publish it. The fact that you are reading it shows that the *end* for me did not come before I was finished writing it. Even as you are reading this book your *end* can come before you are finished reading this page. Praise God my *end* did not come before I was finished writing it. It is not our good fortune to decide when the *end* should be. Some people after years of illness pray for the *end* to come. Some even seek euthanasia to bring about the *end*, and something goes wrong and the *end* does not come. On the other hand one may be in very good health, come from a family that is credited with longevity and the *end* may come while one is in the prime of one's life. This is so because our times are not in our own hands. We hear of persons in the sanctity of their homes being killed by invaders, or worse yet by their own relatives. Recently a mother and father were killed at the hands of their own son. A grandmother was at dinner when her grandson ended her life. There was an incident when a young woman was preparing for a holiday when a stray bullet went through her window and ended her life. There were incidents when persons retired to bed and their lives ended while in bed, either by murder, fire or some other reason. There is no certainty that once we are in the comfort of our homes that we will live to see the next day

Just to emphasize again that there is no certainty to living let me point out this fact. One can be the best driver, just receive a clean bill of health from the doctor and joyfully on the way to the next destination, observing all the rules of the road, when suddenly tragedy can strike. The other driver on the road may be either overcome with bad news, become ill, or high on some restricted substance and comes crashing into the vehicle of the safe driver. And, before one can say 'Lord, have mercy on my soul', the *end* comes. We in the United States have seen first- hand, with the events of 9/11, that there is no guarantee to life on this earth.

What have we learnt from what has been stated? We can say without a doubt that we have learnt that our lives are not in our hands. The question is 'In whose hands are our lives?' I can say emphatically that our lives are not in the hands of mankind. Our lives are in God's hands: let us enjoy having them in His hands, so that we would not have to be using many 'If's', especially *'if I had known I would have lived a Godly life'*

The Unending Possibilities of 'If'

When one encounters pleasant or unpleasant experiences one begins to think of a series of possibilities. If I had known the returns on the investment would have been so good I would have invested more money or if I had known that the investment was not good I would not have invested so much money. If I were born at a different time ... If I were born of a different racial back ground ... If I were born into a different economic status ... If I were born in a different State, Country, Region ... If my parents, employer, friend etc did do or did not do ... If my spouse did or did not do ... If Adam and Eve did or did not ... ... if, if, if, if, if, if ... ... If we prepare for leaving this earth we could look forward to that *DAY* with great expectation.

Those of us who prepare for death may find that we may not taste death, but could be taken. The Bible says that Enoch, who was three hundred and sixty five years, *"walked with God: and he was not; for God took him."* Genesis 5:24.   In *Hebrews 11:5* we read *"By faith Enoch was translated that he should not see death; and was not found, because God had translated him: for before his translation he had this testimony, that he pleased God."* Another man of God left this earth without seeing death. 2 *Kings 2:11 states "And it came to pass, as they still went on, and talked, that behold, there appeared a chariot of fire, and horses of fire and parted them both asunder; and Elijah went up by a whirlwind into heaven."*

From the examples we see that there were persons, who left this earth without tasting death. We too can leave this earth without tasting death if the Lord comes now for His chosen. However if we leave this earth before He comes we do not have to worry; as it is stated in 1 *Thessalonians 4:16 "For the Lord himself shall descend from heaven with a shout, with voice of the archangel, and with the trump of God: and the dead in Christ shall rise first:"*

From what is recorded in the scriptures death is not something to be feared or ignored. It is an event for which we should prepare. Some people have been preparing for death in a physical sense. Some have established pre-paid burial plans, and have paid off their funeral expenses, so that their loved ones would not have to be financially burdened when their *end* comes. Some have even prepared their funeral programs, so that the songs, which they like, would be sung. That is very good. Some have made their wills so that their earthly possessions could be distributed, as they wish, after they depart. But are we preparing for Eternity? Are we considering the options of Eternity and preparing for the better place, Heaven?

Eternity is defined in the Webster Dictionary as an 'indefinite time. Eternal existence as contrasted with mortal life.' Eternity is associated with a promise of everlasting life. The very important question is where will we spend this eternal/everlasting life? One can spend everlasting life enduring the experience of eternal fire, as is recorded in *Revelation 20:10* *"And the devil that deceived them was cast into the lake of fire and brimstone, where the beast and the false prophet are, and shall be tormented day and night forever and ever."*

One can also spend Eternity enjoying Eternal life, with Jesus, who said *"To him that overcometh will I grant to sit with me in my throne, even as I also overcame, and am set down with my Father in his throne"* Revelation 3:21 Some of us may say 'If it is possible I would like to spend eternity with God'. I say boldly *it is possible.*

The Complexity of IF

The dictionary defines *if* as a 'conjunction meaning in case that: used to introduce an exclamatory phrase, qualifications or excuses.' As we see from its definition, *if*, though a very small word can be used under various situations. It is a word that can conjure up extreme happiness. It is a word that can conjure up extreme sadness. It is a word that can motivate us to immense prosperity and it is a word that can lead us to extreme poverty. It is also a word that can motivate us to have a closer walk with God as we entertain the possibility of spending Eternity with Him.

HAPPINESS

If, as it relates to happiness: A young woman can think thus 'If I were to meet my Prince Charming I would marry him and live happily ever after.' Such a thought can influence that young woman to conduct herself in such a way, that when she meets her Prince Charming there would be no skeletons in her closet that would prevent him from marrying her. With that thought in mind she will walk around with a hopeful joy in her heart as she waits to meet her Prince Charming. On the other hand there can be day dreaming, which can lead to disaster. A Western fable is told of a milk maid, who day dreamed of what she would she would do when she sold the milk she was carrying on her head, and began skipping and dancing; and down fell the milk, which brought her back to reality. At least for a moment she enjoyed much happiness.

SADNESS

Some of us can cause ourselves to experience immeasurable sadness by our *IF* thoughts. For instance one may think 'If I were to go to work and receive a pink slip it would cause me to be so sad, as I would have no means of paying my bills and supporting myself and family. I will be thrown out of my house and would have nowhere to live. I would have either to live in a shelter or go and ask lodging with relatives or friends. This would be very embarrassing'. Such sad thoughts could cause one to be so depressed that one could become ill and indeed be laid off, not because of downsizing but because ill health/absenteeism, caused by the negative thoughts which one allowed to occupy one's mind. Sometimes negative *IF* thoughts cause some to become reclusive which may intensify depression.

PROSPERITY

One day a young man said to himself, 'If I can only invest these few dollars, which I have, I would be able to supplement my income'. Buying and selling candy, and diligently managing his money he saw that over time, he not only supplemented his income, but he was able to employ others to assist him, as he expanded the commodities he bought and sold. Today he is a successful businessman. It is easy to associate oneself with positive *IF* stories.

POVERTY

An individual hears of the man, who went to the casino and struck it rich. He said if I can win that money all of my problems would be over. I would not have to work again and I would be able to live the 'good life.' He starts his gambling exploits. He wins a little. He is encouraged. He loses a little, he is hopeful. He loses big. He is still hopeful. He is so set in his dreams that he borrows, and then steals in order to strike it rich. He ends up, not only a pauper, but in jail.

Walk with God

We must walk with God if we want our desire of spending Eternity with Him to be realized. Not only that, but there are other things which will happen. Jesus has said in *Matthew 6:33 "seek ye first the kingdom of God, and His righteousness; and all these things shall be added you."* Let me state right here and now that God gives us what we need, so *all things* must be seen relative to our needs. God will not give the man, who lives in the tropics a winter coat, snow boots, gloves and winter hats. He does not have need for that. He will give him, as He will give all of us, what he needs. God's provision of our needs can be financial or they can be gifts from individuals. Happiness would be ours as we demonstrate satisfaction with what God provides. *Psalm 144:15 encourages "Happy is that people, that is in such a case: yea, happy is that people, whose God is the Lord."* Prosperity would be ours; as is stated in *2 Chronicles 26:5 "And he sought God in the days of Zechariah, who had understanding in the visions of God: and as long as he sought the Lord, God made him to prosper".* Sadness would be taken care of as Jesus was sent *"to bind up the broken hearted, to proclaim liberty to the captives, and the opening of the prison to them that are bound." Isaiah 61:1.* Poverty would not be ours even if we do not become billionaires, for David states in *Psalm 37: 25 "I have been young, and now am old; yet have I not seen the righteous forsaken, nor his seed begging bread."*

Let us now focus on one of the *If* that is often used, especially when faced with life's challenges. *'If Adam and Eve did or did not.'* Let us go to the Bible to see what Adam and Eve did or did not do.

Genesis chapter 2:7 states "And the Lord God formed man of the dust of the ground, and breathed into his nostrils the breath of life; and man became a living soul." In the same chapter verses 15- 17 we read thus *"And the Lord God took the man, and put him into the Garden of Eden to dress it and to* keep it. And the Lord God commanded the man, saying, Of every tree of the garden thou mayest freely eat: But of the tree of the knowledge of good and evil, thou shalt not eat of it: for in the day that thou eatest thereof thou shalt surely die." (Please note that Adam was told what would be the result of his choice. Most of us have some idea of what would be the results of the choices we make.)

Genesis 2:21-25 states "the Lord God caused a deep sleep to fall upon Adam, and he slept: and he took one of his ribs, and closed up the flesh instead thereof. And the rib, which the Lord God had taken from man, made he a woman, and brought her unto the man. And Adam said, This is now bone of my bones, and flesh of my flesh: she shall be called Woman, because she was taken out of Man. And they were both naked, the man and his wife, and were not ashamed."

We note in Genesis 3:4-7 that the woman was given advice contrary to what her husband had been told by God and acted upon it. "And the serpent said unto the woman, Ye shall not surely die: for God doth know that in the day ye eat thereof, then your eyes shall be opened, and ye shall be as gods, knowing good and evil. And when the woman saw that the tree was good for food, and that it was pleasant to the eyes, and a tree to be desired to make one wise, she took of the fruit thereof, and did eat, and gave also unto her husband with her; and he did eat. And the eyes of them both were opened, and they knew they were naked; and they sewed fig leaves together, and made themselves aprons."

The effects of disobedience are shown in Genesis 3:8-15 which states: "And they heard the voice of the Lord walking in the garden in the cool of the day: and Adam and his wife hid themselves from the presence of the Lord God amongst the trees of the garden. And the Lord called unto Adam, and said unto him, 'Where art thou?' And he said, I heard thy voice in the garden, and I was afraid, because I was naked; and I hid myself. And He said who told thee that thou wast naked? Hast thou eaten of the tree, whereof I commanded thee that thou shouldest not eat? And the man said, The woman whom thou gavest to be with me, she gave me of the tree, and I did eat." And the Lord said unto the woman, What is this that thou hast done? And the woman said, The serpent beguiled me, and I did eat. And the Lord God said unto the serpent, Because thou hast done this, thou art cursed above all cattle, and above every beast of the field; upon thy belly thou shalt go, and dust shalt thou eat all the days of thy life: And I will put enmity between thee and the woman, and between thy seed and her seed; it shall bruise thy head, and thou shalt *bruise his heel."* Many theologians state that, at this stage, the awesome responsibility of our Lord and Savior Jesus Christ became evident.

God then pronounced mankind's reward for having disobeyed Him. Genesis 3:16-19 states *"Unto the woman he said, I will greatly multiply thy sorrow and thy conception; in sorrow thou shalt bring forth children; and thy desire shall be to thy husband, and he shall rule over thee. And unto Adam he said, Because thou hast hearkened unto the voice of thy wife, and hast eaten of the tree, of which I commanded thee, saying, Thou shalt not eat of it: cursed is the ground for thy sake; in sorrow shalt thou eat of it all the days of thy life; Thorns also and thistles shall it bring forth to thee; and thou shalt eat the herb of the field: in the sweat of they face shalt thou eat bread, till thou return unto the ground; for out of it wast thou taken: for dust thou art, and unto dust shalt thou return."* From that first demonstration of disobedience (sin) there was disobedience continually throughout the Bible by God's chosen people.

Reality Check

Not everyone believes in the Bible (King James Version), from which I have been quoting or in God as a matter of fact. However, whether or not one believes in the Bible or in God, that does not cause God to be non- existent.

The Atheist resolutely says there is no God. To my fellow human beings, who hold that view I ask you to reconsider your position. The man who is color blind (a condition that is professionally called Color Vision Deficiencies), and says a violet object is blue does not make that violet object blue by stating it is blue. Even if we got as many colorblind individuals, as we can, and put them together to call the violet color blue, that does not make that violet blue. In the same light if a multitude of individuals says there is no God that does not cause God to become non- existent.

The one, who refuses to believe that there is a God because he does not see Him, does not prove that God is not there. We do not see the wind but we breathe in fresh air so that we can remain healthy and alive. Any one, who is deprived of fresh air for a significant period of time, will experience the consequence. He/she becomes either brain damaged or dies. However although we do not see the air, we do not say there is no air. Individuals who fly kites do not see the breeze but we rely on the breeze to keep the kites in the air. We see the trees swaying quite a lot, and without seeing anything we say there is a strong wind. Carbon Monoxide is colorless, odorless and tasteless, yet a highly toxic gas. In the same light we do not see God, in whom some of us believe, but we know that He is present.

We all benefit from the goodness of God whether or not we acknowledge Him. The sky is held in place without any input from man and we all are able to admire it the sun, the moon and the stars. It is God who does that. The snow comes down up earth without man's intervention. It is God. The ocean is continuously filled with water so that man, who has nothing to do with it can plan to go on cruises months in advance without fear that there would be no water for the cruise ships to sail on. It is God. The trees in the jungle grow without any input from man; but man can make a business out of cutting down the trees for lumber or coal. It is God. Sea food is present in the sea, without man's aid. It is God. Birds, animals and other creatures exist, without man's help. It is God. As a matter of fact, man's actions negatively affect these creatures and the environment; that man now has to set out to correct that situation. Various organizations have come into being to prevent these animals/creatures from becoming extinct, and the environment from becoming polluted.

Blessings

There are certain general blessings which God offers to all mankind, whether or not they acknowledge that He exists. God lets the sun shine on all, when day breaks. He lets the moon give its light to all, Believer or not. He lets the rain fall on all, even if some vehemently deny His existence. He lets all enjoy the freshness of his breeze, which no one, who wants to live refuses to breathe whether or not they believe in Him. Those who like to go on cruises may deny there is a God, even while the ship is on the ocean and they are looking up at a full moon and twinkle stars in the sky. They still enjoy the benefits of the ocean. When snow falls, men either praise or curse God depending on what activity they had planned for the day the snow fell. Those who make lots of money removing the snow are happy. Those who like to ski are extremely happy, at the prospect of having much fun. Some, may, even at the same time be denying that there is a God.

God, however, has His special blessings reserved for those who love and trust in Him. He blesses them with *"love, joy, peace, long-suffering, gentleness, goodness, faith, meekness and temperance." (fruit of the Spirit),* Galatians 5:21,22. To the Atheist I say, regardless of your unwillingness to acknowledge that there is a God, one day you will die and you will have to account for your stewardship on this earth. I pray that before that time comes you will accept that there is a God and serve Him.

Jesus

Some acknowledge that there is a God but do not believe in His Son Jesus Christ, as the Savior of all. I encourage you today, to know that God's word says that *"Neither is there salvation in any other; for there is none other name under heaven given among men, whereby we must be saved".* Acts 4:12.One may be serving God in whatever way or form one feels pleased. However, unless you are serving Him in a form where Jesus Christ is the center of your life, you are not preparing to spend Eternity with God, for Romans 8:34 states *"It is Christ that died, yea rather, that is risen again, who is even at the right hand of God, who also maketh intercession for us".* Many have gods whom they believe in but those gods died and have not risen from their graves. Some gods are idols, and *Psalm 115:4 -8 states "their idols are silver and gold, the work of men's hands. They have mouths, but they speak not: eyes have they, but they see not: they have ears, but they hear not: noses have they, but they smell not: they have hands, but they handle not: feet have they but they walk not; neither speak they through their throat. They that make them are like unto them; and so is everyone that trusteth in them".*

Let us understand who Jesus is and what He did. In Isaiah 7:14 we read *"Behold a virgin shall conceive, and bear a son, and shall call his name Immanuel."* This prophecy was fulfilled in .Matthew 1:18-23

"Now the birth of Jesus Christ was on this wise: When as His mother Mary was espoused to Joseph, before they came together, she was found with child of the Holy Ghost. Then Joseph her husband, being a just man, and not willing to make her a public example, was minded to put her away privily. But while he thought on these things, behold, the angel of the Lord appeared unto him in a dream, saying, Joseph, thou son of David, fear not to take unto thee Mary thy wife: for that which is conceived in her is of the Holy Ghost. And she shall bring forth a son, and thou shalt call his name JESUS: for he shall save his people from their sins. Now all this was done, that it might be fulfilled

which was spoken of the Lord by the prophet, saying, 'BEHOLD A VIRGIN SHALL BE WITH CHILD, AND SHALL BRING FORTH A SON, AND THEY SHALL CALL HIS NAME IMMANUEL, which being interpreted is, God with us."

Many great men and women have graced the face of this earth, but none had a miraculous birth like our Lord and Savior. None, has it ever been said, was worthy to save sinners. *Revelation 5:1-9 states " And I saw in the right hand of Him that sat on the throne a book written within and on the back side, sealed with seven seals. And I saw a strong angel proclaiming with a loud voice, 'Who is worthy to open the book, and to lose the seals thereof?' And no man in heaven, nor in earth, neither under the earth, was able to open the book, neither to look thereon. And I wept much, because no man was found worthy to open and to read the book, neither to look thereon. And one of the elders saith unto me, Weep not: behold, the Lion of the tribe of Judah, the Root of David, hath prevailed to open the book, and to loose the seven seals thereof....... And they sung a new song, saying, Thou art worthy to take the book, and to open the seals thereof: for thou wast slain, and hast redeemed us to God by thy blood out of every kindred, and tongue, and people, and nation"*.

One may be making progress in this life. One may be acquiring many riches and may be feeling very comfortable in life, but if Jesus is not the center of it all, that person is in trouble. The Bible asks the question *"For what shall it profit a man, if he shall gain the whole world and lose his own soul? Or what shall a man give in exchange for his soul?"* Mark 8:36-37.

We read of the story of the rich man, who was told *"This night thy soul shall be required of thee."* Luke 12:20. That fact faces each and every one of us, whether rich or poor. Accepting Jesus as the Son of God is the key to our preparation for spending Eternity with God. Even when we pray we are to ask everything of God through Jesus Christ. Someone once said that when we obey and submit our prayers through Jesus Christ, it is as if we have put the stamp on the prayer. When we drop a mail in the post without the stamp it goes nowhere.

Some may say that they have prayed many times without going through Jesus and their prayers have been answered. I do not doubt that. The one who steals and taps himself/herself on his/her back at not being caught will one day realize that he/she cannot continue like that, and unless that individual stops doing wrong he/she will one day face the long arm of the law. It is the same way with God. *Ephesians 4:28 states "Let* him that stole steal no more: but rather let him labor, working with his hands the thing which is good, that he may have to give to him that needeth." God is "a God ready to pardon, gracious and merciful, slow to anger, and of great kindness." Nehemiah 9:17. However, one day God will say 'come home', and you will stand before the Him. What will your answer be when He asks you 'Why did you reject My Son'?

To the one who acknowledges that there is a God, believes that Jesus is the Son of God, but feels that he/she is not ready to make the commitment, I say to you that time is not on your side as tomorrow is promised to no man. Hebrews 3:15 "today if you will hear his voice, harden not your hearts, as in the provocation." We may have been born into a family, whose members have lived long lives; however there is no guarantee that we will live to a ripe old age.

To the one, who has accepted Jesus Christ as the Son of God and our Lord and Savior, has been baptized and goes to church, I say congratulation. I pray that you will understand that you have entered into the most serious relationship of your life, and that you will cherish that relationship more than anything else on this earth. This is the relationship that guarantees us a happy Eternity. This relationship has to be worked on, on a daily basis, as "your adversary the devil, as a roaring lion, walketh about, seeking whom he may devour." 1 Peter5:8.

One may ask, why is all this necessary for me to spend Eternity with God. I am a good person and come from a very good family.

We serve a God, who loved us so much, that "He gave his only begotten Son, that whosoever believeth in Him should not perish, but have everlasting life." (John 3:16) We must acknowledge that we "all have sinned, and come short of the glory of God." Romans 3:23 We may not know what sin we might have done, as we feel that we have been good all the days of our lives. However because we are descendants from the first man, Adam, who was disobedient to God and sinned, we all have the sin nature in our being. One has to ask God to lead him/her to a church, where His word is taught in spirit and in truth. Upon hearing the word of God, one must make a commitment to live for Him. One must repent of one's sins, which will become very clear as one reads the Bible.

Some may feel that they have done so many terrible things that God would not want them. Be encouraged, that that is far from the character of God, who has said in Isaiah 1:18 "though your sins be as scarlet, they shall be as white as snow; though they be red like crimson, they shall be as wool."

Those of you, who are reading this book, and have had the experience of witnessing fresh snow on the ground, know how white and beautiful it is. The cotton wool in the bottle that holds solid medication is white. Imagine the miracle, of our sin stained lives, becoming so white, in the sight of a holy God. That is the beauty of Salvation. We have a chance to start life without any blemish. Man may not forget the bad things, we may have done; however, the One who matters most, Almighty God, who holds our destiny in His hands, will forgive us once we repent and ask Him for forgiveness. Praise God for His love towards us.

You may ask 'what exactly is repentance and how is this possible?' The Webster Dictionary defines repentance as "deep sorrow for past sin or wrong doing". We sin against God, and He sees our hearts and can accept our sorrowful hearts and forgive us. When repentance is accompanied by a sincere desire to turn from our old ways, and to surrender our lives to God, there is where the miracle occurs. That is when we become the new person. 2 Cor. 5:17 states: "*Therefore if any man be in Christ, he is a new creature: old things are passed away; behold all things are become new.*"

After repenting and acknowledging that Jesus' life was given for you, seek to learn more about Him. Familiarize yourself with what He says you must do in order to enter into God's Kingdom. This is what He says in *John 3:3* "*Verily, Verily I say unto thee, Except a man be born again, he cannot see the kingdom of God.*" Again He says: "*Except a man be born of water and of the Spirit, he cannot enter into the kingdom if God.*" *John 3:5.* You must be baptized, by immersion, when Jesus, who is our *Example*, went to be baptized of John the Baptist, John said "*I have need to be baptized of thee, and comest thou to me?*" *Matthew 3:14.* Jesus seeing his reluctance said "*Suffer it to be so now: for thus it becometh us to fulfill all righteousness.*" *Matthew 3:15.* When we obey that command, and follow Jesus' example of baptism, by immersion in water, we do what pleases God. *Matthew 3: 16 -17* states "*And Jesus, when he was baptized, went up straightway out of the water: and, lo, the heavens were opened unto him, and he saw the Spirit of God descending like a dove, and lighting upon him: and lo a voice from heaven, saying, this is my beloved Son, in whom I am well pleased.*"

THE CHRISTIAN WALK

I will now focus on those, of us, who believe in God and His Son Jesus Christ and have been baptized, like Jesus by immersion, and what is expected of us after that step. The Bible is our source on how to conduct ourselves after this wonderful rebirth. *1Peter 2:2 states: "As newborn babes, desire the sincere milk of the word, that ye may grow thereby."* The word of God will tell us what to do, and what not to do, as we operate in our various roles in the life. Any time we act in a way that is contrary to what the Bible says, we sin and we jeopardize our chance of entering into Eternity with Christ, if our *end* comes before we have been able to repent of our sins. Let me state, emphatically, the reason why Jesus came, it was not of us to have the nice things in life. His reason for coming was for us to have eternal life.

Yes, there are promises in the Bible of prosperity, healing blessings and all the many promises that are recorded. However, these are *off shoots* of living a life prepared for Eternity.

History has shown that many children of God have lived lives dangerously, by having secret sins. David spoke thus in *Psalm 19: 12-13 "Who can understand his errors? Cleanse thou me from secret faults. Keep back thy servant also from presumptuous sins; let them not have dominion over me: then shall I be upright, and I shall be innocent from the great transgression."*

Often we embrace the fact, that we have an Advocate in Jesus, as indicated in 1John 2:1, which states: *"My little children, these things write I unto you, that ye sin not. And if any man sin, we have an advocate with the Father, Jesus Christ the righteous."* I would like to state firmly, that before one can advocate for someone, the person has to tell the advocate his/her problem. If persons die in their sins there is nothing the advocate can do with regards to approaching God on behalf of the dead.

Usually, before persons tell advocates their problems, they exchange pleasantries. We, as Believers, before we send our petitions to our Advocate, must worship and praise Him. However if we are taken away suddenly in our sins, there is nothing we can do as *Psalm 115:17 states: "The dead praise not the Lord, neither any that go down into silence."*

As we do not know when our *end* will come, according to *Matthew 25:13, which states, Watch therefore, for ye know neither the day nor the hour when the Son of man cometh,"* and under what circumstance, we must strive, with the help of God, to be ready at all times.

SOME SINS THAT EASILY BESET US

I will now focus on some sins, secret or otherwise, which some of us commit, or consider committing, and which we have to make a serious effort to purpose in our hearts that we would not continue to commit or begin to commit any of these sins. Time will not permit me to comment on all the sins recorded in the Bible; however, as we study God's Word, we will become familiar with them, so that we would not continue to, or start to commit them. *Hebrews12:1 advises "Let us lay aside every weight, and the sin which doth so easily beset us, and let us run with patience the race that is set before us."* The dictionary defines beset as 'to attack on all sides'. There is an enemy of our soul, Satan, who seeks to have us disobey God, as he was able to get Adam and Eve to do. We must remember that we have been instructed *"Thou shalt be perfect with the Lord thy God."* *Deuteronomy 18:13.* As we strive for perfection I will list a few of the things we are tempted to do, or do, which may put our spending Eternity with our Lord at risk, if our *end* came suddenly.

ABUSE

> *"What is my reward then? Verily that, when I preach the gospel, I make the gospel of Christ without charge, that I abuse not my power in the gospel." 1 Corinthians 9:18.*

Abuse is described in the Webster Dictionary as 'to use wrongfully or improperly, misuse: to abuse one's authority'. Some of us, who preach the Word of God, whether regularly or occasionally, misuse our authority. Some demand that individuals make contributions to the church, outside of their tithes and offerings, regardless of how these individuals are struggling financially. Some put a psychological guilt on the congregation, indicating how many hours we have to spend in preparation for a sermon, how much time we spend interceding for the congregation and visiting the sick and those in distress. Preachers must be careful. When we take the mike, we must realize that while man hears the words, which they speak, God sees the intent behind those words. Are the words to convict the members of sin and motivate them to strive for a closer walk with God, or are the words intended for them to give until it 'hurts'.

Paul states in *1 Corinthians 9: 18 "when I preach the gospel, I make the Gospel of Christ without charge, that I abuse not my power in the Gospel."* Preachers must be conscious of our intent whenever we sit to prepare a sermon, and when we take the mike. David, who was described as a man after God's heart, admonished his son Solomon thus. *"And thou, Solomon my son, know thou the God of thy father, and serve him with a perfect heart and with a willing mind: for the Lord searcheth all hearts, and understandeth all the imaginations of the thoughts." 1 Chronicles 28:9.*

The preacher's thoughts behind every message must not be for selfish gains, like filthy lucre, *Titus 1: 11 indicates that some individuals "subvert whole houses, teaching things which they ought not, for filthy lucre's sake."* The intention must be to motivate individuals to strive live holy lives. The intention must be to let individuals remember that they were saved to spend eternity with Jesus in heaven. Preachers must be conscious that we are not exempted from living *'perfect'* in the sight of God, even concerning our thoughts. Paul was so conscious of the demand on preachers that he said in *1 Corinthians 9:27 "But I keep under my body, and bring it into subjection: lest that by any means, when I have preached to others, I myself should be a cast away."* Preachers must live by the very word we preach. One preacher, who is alleged to have had the knack of raising funds, was invited to a church to preach on giving. He convicted people who were not tithing to amend their ways and even to repay what they had robbed God of. *"The people responded to the minister's message and gave more than $60.000 in offering. Following the service, this minister told the pastor of the church that the entire offering should go to him, not the church. 'You will be blessed by sowing this offering into my ministry', the pastor was told."*(The blessed life by Robert Morris page 125). Where do you think that pastor would have spent eternity if his *end* had come immediately after collecting his cash? I wish all preachers will remember this: Preachers must note that what we tell the congregation from God's Word: *"my God shall supply all your need according to his riches in glory by Christ Jesus." Philippians 4:19;* is not just for the persons sitting in the pews, it is also for the preachers. So we do not have to abuse *our* authority.

Some Believers, who are not preachers, also indulge in abuse. Some verbally, physically, sexually, emotionally or otherwise abuse others. Some do it behind closed doors. Some spouses, after they are abused, put on lots of makeup and wear dark glasses to camouflage the abuse. Some persons take pleasure in abusing the disadvantaged. Some abuse also comes in the form of exploitation, whereby some employers work persons to stump and pay them next to nothing. *Be careful, be very careful.* Believers must realize that while abusing someone, or immediately after abusing man, woman or child the *end* can come and seal the abuser's fate to an Eternity away from Christ.

ADULTERY

"Thou shalt not commit adultery"."Exodus 20:14

Adultery is an act, which is usually committed in secrecy. The Webster Dictionary defines adultery as 'voluntary sexual intercourse between a married person and someone other than his or her lawful spouse.' Many persons, when they commit adultery, find lots of excuses to justify the acts, such they were loneliness, weakness, desires/ needs, and temptation by the other person. Some say God would understand why the sin was committed. It is important to note that none of our excuses for adultery would be accepted by God. Adultery is so serious an offence that *1 Corinthians 6:9 states "Know ye not that the unrighteous shall not inherit the kingdom of God? Be not deceived: neither fornicators, nor idolaters, nor adulterers."* Jesus in speaking about adultery, let His disciples know that, without even committing a physical act, one can still commit adultery when He said in *Matthew 5:28 "I say unto you, that whosoever looketh on a woman to lust after her hath committed adultery with her already in his heart."* Sometimes women dress in very seductive garments and men stare after them until they are out of their view. Only God knows what thoughts pass through their minds, as they stare after the females. Lest it seem as only men stare after women, women also fanaticize after males, who have well built physiques. Let us therefore be mindful of how we use our thoughts, as our *end* can come while we are in an adulterous state, whether physically or mentally.

With respect to adultery, when it pleases society they frown upon it with much partiality. Recently a famous sportsman committed adultery and the media and some of his financial backers chastised him, while the females, allegedly involved, were glorified. In another instant a governor who committed adultery resigned his position and was demonized in the media, while the woman involved, said she had been given a position, with a newspaper, to write about relationships and sex. In another instance a woman who had an adulterous relationship with a 2008 Presidential candidate, and bore him a child, was so proud that she wrote a book and was embraced by the media.

It has been said that the hands that rock the cradle rule the world. The world will be in a very sad state, if the bodies to which those hand are attached commit adultery without any shame. We all must be very careful as while mankind is selective in whom they choose to chastise for wrong doing, our God, who sees and knows everything will judge each and every one of us for our actions, whether or not society approves of them.

One may say those who were involved in those incidents were not Christians. If that were so, they may be in a better place than Christians, as their Christian friends may be praying for them to change their ways. However the Christian, whether Pastor or church member; who is secretly committing adultery, is in serious trouble as no one would be praying for them to change their ways and may leave this earth while in their adulterous situation, even in the very act. However, while I do not know the spiritual standing of the persons who commit adultery, there are some professed Christians, who do. Recently a Presidential Candidate, who is said to be a Baptist Minister, had to end his political career because he was accused of groping women and carrying on an adulterous affair with another woman for a number of years. Well known pastors have had to take leave of absence because of committing adultery. We are all tempted to do various things which are against God's will. However we have a promise in.*1 Corinthians 10:13"There hath no temptation taken you but such as is common to man: but God is faithful, who will not suffer you to be tempted above that ye are able; but will with the temptation also make a way to escape, that ye may be able to bear it."* May God help us to find that way of escape, or may the Holy Spirit convict us, so we may repent immediately.

ARROGANCE

"The fear of the Lord is to hate evil: pride, and arrogancy, and the evil way, and the forward mouth, do I hate." Proverb 8:13.

Arrogance is defined as an 'offensive display of superiority or self importance, overbearing pride, haughtiness'. Arrogance, when displayed by the unbeliever offends mankind; when displayed by the Believer, it offends man and displeases God. It is necessary for us to be cognizant of the fact that arrogance is offensive to God.

Sometimes, some of us, Christians hear about the shortcomings of other Christians, whether real or perceived, and we display an arrogant attitude towards the alleged weak ones. We treat them with disdain. We shun them and exclude them from activities *reserved for the righteous.* We, who may consider ourselves strong, must be very mindful of what the scripture says in *Galatians 6:1 "Brethren, if a man be overtaken in a fault, ye which are spiritual, restore such a one in the spirit of meekness; considering thyself, lest thou also be tempted."* The alleged erring individuals, we hear about, may commit sins which are seen by the natural eyes, but judgmental individuals may commit sins, which are seen by the eyes of God. Let us all therefore be very careful how we react to things we hear about others.

Some Believers may enjoy more material success than others and may adopt an arrogant attitude, flaunting their material goods, and talking down to those, who have not received their blessings as yet. We must be very mindful how we deal with anything that is physical. These things can vanish in a moment. In the recent pass we have seen homes, multi- million dollars homes, or humble dwellings, destroyed by fire, tornadoes, floods and other natural disasters. We have seen wealthy individuals become poor due to dishonest persons who rob them of their wealth. Due to mishandling of their fortune, or indulging in habits, which are detrimental to their bodies and their pockets, some persons lose their economic status. History is full of persons, men, powerful men, and women who sometimes were arrogant, during their moments of fame, but when they fell from grace they sought the forsaken ones to comfort them. Let us ask God to help us that arrogance would not be found among us, as we prepare to spend Eternity with Him.

BACKSLIDE

Jeremiah 2:19 states "Thine own wickedness shall correct thee, and they backslidings shall reprove thee: know therefore and see that it is an evil thing and bitter, that thou has forsaken the Lord thy God, and that my fear is not in thee, saith the Lord God of host."

The dictionary defines *backslide* as 'to relapse into bad habits, sinful behavior or undesirable behaviors.' The New Ungers Bible Dictionary describes backsliding as ' being stubborn or refactory life of a heifer, turning back to the old life of sin and idolatry, a change in the Believer's state before God, but not of His standing'. Sometimes after we give our hearts to God, we may encounter challenges in life. We may reflect on the life we lived before; without any constraint, getting what we wanted, when we wanted it, regardless of how we got it. We might even consider returning to that life, for a short while *until things are straightened out.* Sometimes Believers do not physically return immediately, but would return mentally, often thinking about it until we eventually return to our old sinful ways.

Some Believers may even be in the church and indulge in acts that are not pleasing in the sight of God. When convicted by the Hoy Spirit, through a sermon we may leave the assembly, using the sermon as the excuse, saying the preacher was targeting us. Unless we repent of our thoughts and ask God to help us to remain steadfast and un-moveable we would be in spiritual trouble. *Proverbs 14:14 states "The backslider in heart shall be filled with his own ways."* Let us be mindful of our thoughts. Whenever we find our thoughts turning to sinful things, of the past, let us ask God to bring us back to Him. Let us remember that God sees even when a sermon is being preached if we are in a backslidden state. We may be in church, just in body, but our minds, may not focusing on anything, which is going on.

While our hearts may be filled with contempt and/or disdain for most persons in the church, we may summon a smile, when we think it is needed. Persons can have hatred in their hearts and still behave as if they love the individuals for whom they harbor the hatred. A Congressman, in New York, once passed a supposed friend around the security metal detector into the Congress Hall, and after he gained entry he killed the very congressman right there. The heart of man is indeed desperately wicked. Persons may offend or hurt us, but let us not sit in the church with evil thoughts, only waiting for a moment to deal with the person and then leave the church. Let us remember that our God with whom we would like to spend Eternity knows our hearts and our *end* can come even while our hearts are not right with God.

CORRUPT

Ephesians 4:29 states *"Let no corrupt communication proceed out of your mouth, but that which is good to the use of edifying, that it may minister grace unto the hearers."* But one may say 'what is corrupt communication?' The dictionary defines corrupt as debased in character, depraved". It is conversation that is morally bad in taste. It is conversation, of which, we would be ashamed of, if someone, who knows us, as Believers, were to overhear. How much more careful should we be, knowing that God hears everything. We must remember that *"those things which proceed out of the mouth come forth from the heart; and they defile the man."* Matthews 15:18.

Sometimes some of us feel that it is OK to speak in a sinful manner, to some persons, because we convince ourselves, that those persons would not behave in the manner, we want them to behave, unless we communicate to them in a manner which, we assume, they only understand; so words of profanity and/or swearing are used. Let us be careful, because we can leave this earth even while those words are coming out of our mouths.

COVETOUSNESS

"Thou shalt not covet thy neighbor's house, thou shalt not covet thy neighbor's wife, nor his manservant, nor his maidservant, nor his ox, nor his ass, nor any thing that is thy neighbor's." Exodus 20:17

Covetous come from the root word covet which the Oxford Dictionary defines as to 'desire eagerly (especially something belonging to another person.)' Some persons when they covet other persons' things they put themselves in further problems in order to get that, which they have coveted. David coveted Uriah's wife and sent him with a letter in which was written *"Set ye Uriah in the forefront of the hottest battle, and retire ye from him, that he may be smitten, and die." 2 Samuel 11:15.* David did that in order to cover up his sinful act, with the woman he had coveted. David, however, found out that nothing is hidden from God, when the prophet, Nathan revealed to him his sin. One may say that David eventually became a great man. Yes, he did, because he was willing and able to repent for his actions. Psalm 51 is one, with which each of us should become familiar. Some individuals harbor covetousness in their hearts, and just wait for an opportunity to get what is coveted. Some may not kill anyone physically, but they may steal, lie to the person or be involved in other schemes to get what is coveted. I think that any time we admire something, that someone has so much, that we are consumed with thoughts of it most of the time, we have crossed over from admiring what the person has, to having a desire to covet it, just awaiting a time when we can possess it. God knows our hearts, and the desires which are raging within. If we can confess to Him and ask Him to help us to overcome such desires He can. Let us do what is necessary so that we can be in right standing if the *end* comes now.

DECEITFUL

> Psalm 5:6 states *"The Lord will abhor the bloody and deceitful man."*

Deceitful, which comes from the root word deceive which means, according to the Webster dictionary, 'to mislead by a false appearance or statement; trick, it suggests hypocrisy or pretense.' The Bible speaks among other things against deceitful balances. Proverbs 11:1 states *"a false balance is abomination to the Lord: but a just weight is his delight."* Some entrepreneurs feel they must maximize their profits by any means. Some tamper with weights, give wrong measurements; some, instead of throwing away expired food items, repackage them and sell them to unsuspecting customers, sometimes causing individuals to become ill. Some misrepresent the value of a commodity and the list goes on. Some of these individuals who do these things are Believers also. Let us remember that once we are saved that does not exempt us from judgment if we violate the commands of God. Some individuals misrepresent facts about themselves so as to get a job or favor from someone. Some tell such convincing stories that even 'smart' people are duped. Let us be careful as the *end* can come even before we able to enjoy the gain, we got by deceit.

DEFILE

> *1 Corinthians 3:16, 17 state "Know ye not that ye are the temple of God, and that the Spirit of God dwelleth in you? If any man defile the temple of God, him shall God destroy; for the temple of God is holy, which temple ye are."*

The dictionary says to defile means 'to desecrate, to make unclean'. We therefore have to keep our temple free from anything that would cause us to sin against God, and so cause our temple to become unholy. This temple is not defiled only by the forbidden substances that are put in it, like drugs, alcohol and poison but also by the thoughts that we harbor within defile us. *Matthew 15:18-19 "Those things which proceed out of the mouth come forth from the heart; and they defile the man. For out of the heart proceed evil thoughts, murders, adulteries, fornications, thefts, false witness, blasphemies."* Let us guard our hearts, and it will be well with our souls, for out of our hearts are the issues of life. Let us remember that while mankind only sees what we show them on the outside, God, who can call us home at any time, or come for us, knows what is in the heart, and if our hearts are not right, we will not be in right standing with Him, and will not be able to spend Eternity with Him.

DESPISE

> *Proverbs 14: 21 states "He that despiseth his neighbor sinneth." Proverbs 23: 22 states "Despise not thy mother when she is old."*

Despise, according to the dictionary is to 'regard with contempt or disdain' It is necessary therefore to treat all individuals with respect. One may say, what must we do, when we interact with individuals, who are not nice? We just have to leave them to God, who has said *"vengeance is mine, I will repay, saith the Lord" Romans 12:19.* With respect to our mothers, whether we, with more knowledge, education and experience than her, feel she did not do her best, with what she had, we never-the –less have to respect her. As a matter of fact, we are commanded to honor her. In Exodus 20:12 children are especially commanded to honor their parents. With peer pressure so prevalent, and many means of communication available, which today give some young people the impression that they are masters of their own destiny, disrespect of parents is sometimes very profound, until young people find themselves in trouble. Sometimes young people show blatant disregard for their teachers, elders and any one in general, as the situation arise. Some individuals disdain others, who are of a lower economic status than them, while smiling, outwardly, with them. Let us be aware of our conduct, as the righteous Judge may be making a serious decision concerning our *end*.

DISOBEDIENCE

Colossians 3:6" "The wrath of God cometh on the children of disobedience."

Disobedience comes from the root word disobey, which is defined as 'to neglect or to refuse'. The Bible is full of instructions on how man should live, in order to please God. *Psalm 119:9 states: Wherewithal shall a young man cleanse his way? By taking heed thereto according to thy word."* A sacred song puts it beautifully 'Trust and obey; for there's no other way to be happy in Jesus, but to trust and obey'. Often preachers neglect to let listeners know or be reminded us, that our God is also a God of wrath, and that He chaseneth even those whom he loves .In 1 Samuel 15 Saul was disobedient to one of God's instructions and said he did, what he did, in order to sacrifice to God. Saul was advised by Samuel *"Behold, to obey is better than sacrifice."* 1 Samuel 15:22. If we, Believers, pursue a disobedient path in our walk with God, we will face the consequences. The worse consequence will be our loss of our place in Eternity with Jesus, if death or the Rapture were to come suddenly before we could repent. We all have been born again and *1John 5:18 states "We know that whosoever is born of God sinneth not; but he that is begotten of God keepeth himself and the wicked one toucheth him not."* Let us guard our salvation which was not bought with silver or gold, but with the precious blood of Jesus.

DISPLEASE

Genesis 38:10 says "And the thing which he did displeased the Lord: wherefore he slew him also."

Displease is defined as 'to incur the dissatisfaction or dislike'
This refers to the situation of Oran as outlined in Genesis 38: 1-10. God's response to our action or in-action, may or may not be as drastic. However, because we do not know how God will discipline us when we displease Him, we should try not to incur his hot displeasure. God's displeasure is spurred by any action that is not generated from a pure heart. Sometimes God may discipline us, in a manner, which gives us an opportunity to repent of the wrong, which we did. In mercy we may suffer loss of our possessions or our health as a form of punishment. In Joshua Chapter 7 when Achan sinned, it caused Israel to suffer defeat. Achan's sin had to be dealt with, in order to have Israel's blessing restored. May God help us that our thoughts, words and actions would always be pleasing to Him.

DIVORCE

Matthew 5:32 states "But I say unto you, that whosoever shall put away his wife, saving for the cause of fornication, causeth her to commit adultery: and whosoever shall marry her that is divorced committeth adultery."

Divorce is defined as 'a judicial declaration dissolving a marriage and releasing both spouses from all matrimonial obligations'. It is said that divorce among Believers is very high, including preachers. We find, that even among Believers, much sin is committed and forgiveness is either absent or abused, thus leading to divorce. I pray that God will help us to live according to his word in Ephesians 5:22-33, which advises husbands and wives how they must live with each other; so that there would be no need for divorces, as harmony would be evident. There was a time when one felt that after seven years of marriage, couples were settled in that marriage for life. However, recently, divorces are occurring between couples, who have been married for over twenty five years, even among preachers. If there is any good in divorces after so many years, it is that there may not be small children, to be destroyed by the trauma of divorce. While a person can be reconciled to God after a divorce, because he is a merciful God, their place with Him in heaven could have been in jeopardy, while they were indulging in the activities, which caused the divorce. Death or the Rapture could have occurred.

ENVY

Genesis 37:11 states "And his brethren envied him."

The dictionary defines envy as 'a feeling of resentful discontent, begrudging admiration, or covetousness with regards to another's advantages, possessions or attainments, desire for something possessed by another'.

We read what happened as result of Joseph's brothers' envy of him. They tried to kill him and by God providence, he was sold instead, and eventually became second in command of Egypt, after many tragic events. *Acts 13:45 states "But when the Jews saw the multitudes, they were filled with envy, and spake against those things which were spoken by Paul, contradicting and blaspheming."*

Envying denotes a longing to possess something awarded to or achieved by another. In some instances envy cripples us from even worshipping genuinely, as we envy the one with the melodious voice, as he/she leads the worship or renders a solo. Envy is such a strong force in one's life, that it causes some to commit sin. Joseph's brothers envied him because of the love his father demonstrated towards him, thought of killing him. King Saul envied David so much that he tried to kill him several times. Envy can cause us to lose the joy that could be ours. Only we can ask God to deliver us from the spirit of envy, as it is such a secret sin, that observers may not know of it, so they are unable to help the person who is experiencing envy. I think one way we can know if we experiencing envy, is when we cannot, from a sincere heart, enjoy what someone is sharing, or compliment someone on an achievement. Let us ask God to help us, so that we could rejoice with those that do rejoice, some of whom we hope to spend Eternity with in heaven, when the *end* comes.

EVILDOER

> Isaiah 31:2 states "Yet he also is wise, and will bring evil, and will not call back his words; but will arise against the house of the evildoers, and against the help of them that work iniquity."

The dictionary defines evildoer as 'a person, who does evil, which is something that is morally wrong, bad immoral and wicked'. Often we look at people, who openly do bad things, and who at the same time seem to be prospering, and fret at their progress, and sometimes feel that life is unfair. While the temptation is very strong to follow the evildoer's actions, we Believers, know that our hope is not only in this world *because* "*if in this life only we have hope in Christ, we are all men most miserable.*" 1 *Corinthians 15:19*. But praise God our hope is in an Eternity away from this earth. Sometimes individuals do evil things to be even with someone who has offended them. However when we give our lives to God we have to let him take care of all that concerns us, as he says in *Romans 12:19* "*Dearly beloved, avenge not yourselves, but rather give place unto wrath: for it is written Vengeance is mine; I will repay, saith the Lord.*" Let us be mindful when we are tempted to take things into our own hands against anyone, as our *end* could come while we are getting even.

FALSE

> Romans 13:9 states "Thou shalt not bear false witness." Proverb 11:1 states "A false balance is abomination to the Lord."

False is defined, in the dictionary as 'not true or correct, uttering or declaring what is untrue, lying, not genuine, counterfeit'. Being involved in anything that is false is an abomination to God. Sometimes we want to present ourselves as what we are not, and we lie. We sometimes soothe our consciences by saying we just told a little 'white lie.' There is no distinction in lying. Business people sometimes talk up a bad commodity and consider themselves to be very smart when they dupe the unsuspecting buyer. Some business people give short measures, in order to extend their profits. The employee, who makes a mistake and fears its consequences sometimes falsify documents, in order to hide the mistake. An old saying goes this way 'Speak the truth and speak it ever, cause it what it will, he who hides the wrong he did does the wrong thing still.' While we may be fooling mankind for a while, we put out Soul's Eternal destination in jeopardy, if our end comes before we have a chance to make right what we did. If we are caught, in whatever dishonest acts we are involved in, we should consider ourselves lucky. While shame or jail may result, things could have been otherwise. We could have been called home in that state of dishonesty. I pray that God will help us to be truthful in all endeavors of life.

FILTHY

"But now ye also put off all these; anger, wrath, malice, blasphemy, filthy communication out of your mouth." Colossians 3:8. Filthy communication is defined as 'vulgar or obscene, contemptible, offensive, vile or objectionable' Often persons would use such language in normal conversation, claiming freedom of speech. However it becomes more pronounced when they are angry. While place is made for anger in the word of God, we are advised *"be ye angry, and sin not, let not the sun go down upon your wrath." Ephesians 4:26* We must realize that what comes out of our mouths can keep us from spending Eternity with Jesus, which is our primary hope in being a Christian. Sometimes in the moment of one being angry and using filthy words one can suffer a heart attack or a stroke or may even die; or the Rapture can occur while those words are coming out of one's mouth. Let us be very careful with our salvation, and our desire to spend Eternity with Jesus.

FORNIFICATION

> 1 Corinthians 6:13 states: "the body is not for fornication, but for the Lord; and the Lord for the body." Also 1 Thessalonians 4:3 states: For this is the will of God, even your sanctification, that ye should abstain from fornication."

The Webster dictionary defines fornication as 'voluntary sexual intercourse between two unmarried persons or two persons not married to each other.' We may look around and see many people committing fornication, and feel that because a multitude is doing so, it is right. The only right thing is what is recorded in God's Word. Sometimes persons are in conjugal relationships for years and have children together. It is advisable that if you are in such a situation that you get married so that your soul would be in good standing with God.

Sometimes when persons are courting, one party may put pressure on the other, to indulge in sex or the relationship will end. As Christians we live by faith, and if we do believe in God, and He has a certain spouse for an individual He will cause it to come to pass; even if one person refuses to commit fornication. Women in particular must realize that if a male, who is courting you, insists on you indulging in fornication or he will leave, let him go, for there is no guarantee that he will not leave, even after he has violated you. In 2 Samuel 13: 1-19 the story is told of Tamar, who was raped by her brother, Amnon, after he had said that he was so much in love with her, and could not do without her. He feigned sickness, and got his father to send her to him and, after he violated her he *"hated her exceedingly; so that the hatred wherewith he hated her was greater than the love, wherewith he loved her. And Amnon said unto her, Arise, be gone….Put now this woman out from me, and bolt the door after her." 2 Samuel 13:15-17*

Fornication often occurs in privacy, especially if it is between two married persons, not married to each other. However, because life is so fragile and individuals have been known to die while having sex, dying during an act of fornication seals one's fate for hell. Let us all remember that we can leave this world at any time even in the very act of fornication. Every time we commit an act of fornication and live, we must thank God for his grace and mercy and repent.

GRIEVE

Mark 3:5 states "And when he had looked round about on them with anger, being grieved for the hardness of their hearts, he saith unto the man 'Stretch forth thine hand'. And he stretched it out: and his hand was restored whole as the other." Not only do we grieve mankind, with the hardness of our hearts, but we can also grieve the Holy Spirit. *Ephesians 4:30 states "Grieve not the Holy Spirit of God, whereby ye are sealed unto the day of redemption,"* But how do we grieve someone? Grieve is defined as 'to feel grief or great sorrow, to distress mentally, cause to feel sorrow'. Each one of us knows how sad we are when we are distressed over a situation. Let us ask God to help us, not to grieve each other, especially the Holy

Spirit. When we grieve an individual, that person separates himself or herself from us. Sometimes relationships become very strained and some persons are very sad. The grieved party may ask some mutual person to intervene in order to bring the parties together again. However when we grieve the Holy Spirit we are the losers; as the Holy Spirit stops communicating with us, and we become vulnerable to the wiles of the devil, who is desirous of having us sin against God, so that we can be with him when we leave this earth.

HOMOSEXUALITY

> *Romans 1:26- 27 state "For this cause God gave them up unto vile affections: for even their women did change the natural use into that which is against nature: And likewise also the men, leaving the natural use of the woman, burned in their lust one toward another; men with men working that which is unseemly, and receiving in themselves that recompense of their error which was meet."*

That lifestyle is described as homosexuality, which is defined as 'sexual attraction towards members of one own sex; sexual activity with another of the same sex.' In Genesis 19:1-29, we see such behavior was demonstrated in Sodom, and that once great city was destroyed. Homosexual lifestyle may be becoming popular and glorified, because of the status in society of some of the persons, who are reported in the news, as practicing in such a life style. As with fornication, homosexuality is sometimes indulged in, in secret. Members of clergy have been accused of indulging in homosexual activities and either had to leave the pulpit or compensate individuals who claimed they had homosexual relationship with them. Some States have legalized marriage between homosexual individuals. God's word is the only source, where we can find out what is right or wrong. Any Believer, who remembers why we all gave our lives to Jesus, must remember that sin, in whatever form, will keep us from entering into Eternity with Jesus.

HYPOCRISY

Paul in 1 Timothy 4:1, 2 states that " in the latter times some shall depart from the faith, giving heed to seducing spirits, and doctrines of devils; speaking lies in hypocrisy; having their conscience seared with a hot iron". 1Peter, 2:1 states lay "aside all malice, and all guile, and hypocrisy and envies, and all evil speakings".

Hypocrisy, is described as 'the false profession of desirable or publicly approved qualities, beliefs or feelings; a pretense of having virtues, moral principles or religious beliefs that one does not really possess'. While being a hypocrite may cause persons to feel that they are smart, and may even lend to them being popular for a time, they are putting their place at the Marriage Supper, with the Lamb, in jeopardy, as hypocrisy is lying and lying is sin. It may only be a matter of time before one's deceit is found out: and one may become distraught at being ostracized, and may even commit a worse sin, suicide, as the hypocrite may not be able to bear the results, of having the mask of deceit ripped off. Let us all remember that we can fool mankind; but God is all seeing and all knowing. If the *end* comes while we are in a deceitful state our Eternity in hell is sealed, as there is no repentance in the grave.

INIQUITY

Psalm 66:18 states "If I regard iniquity in my heart the Lord will not hear me." Isaiah 59:2 states "But your iniquities have separated between you and your God, and your sins have hid his face from you, that he will not hear."

Iniquity is defined as 'gross injustice or wickedness, a violation of right or duty, wicked act' . Iniquity can even be the thought before the act. Sometimes individuals are deprived of committing the wicked act, they wanted to commit because of some interruption or a lack of opportunity. Let us assume, someone had decided to sexually assault a minor, but someone prevented such an assault from occurring, because that individual entered the environment, before the assault could have happened. That thought was already there, and God saw that thought.

Unless that wrong doer repents, and asks God to forgive him/her for the desire to commit such an act, he/she is still in the gall of bitterness.

We all might have entertained thoughts of committing some act that was against God Word, regardless of how small it was. It may be a plan not to go somewhere, nor do something, which was asked of us; and then lie about it, to justify our absence or non-action. However, the activity might have been cancelled, and we did not have the opportunity to tell our lie. We are still in trouble, as the liar's seed had already been sown in our heart, and we need to repent, just as if we had actually had the opportunity to tell the lie. We must remember that God sees the imagination of our hearts. We all would like to walk on those streets of gold when our *end* comes. Therefore let us strive to have our lives free of iniquity.

JUDGE

"Judge not, and ye shall not be judged; condemn not, and ye shall not be condemned: forgive and ye shall be forgiven."
Luke 6:37

The dictionary defines judge as 'to infer, think or hold as opinion.' Sometimes we are in the habit of inferring or forming opinions, about others or their actions or words. Most times it is in a negative way. Though our opinions may be wrong, we are so confident about them, that we sometimes share them with others, as if there were facts. Sometimes our actions cause much hurt to the individuals about whom we formed the opinion. As we judge others we may make decisions that can cause us to lose our blessings. God may send an insignificant looking individual to give us a word of wisdom, but because the person is who he/she is, we do not take what is said seriously and suffer the consequences. May God help us, not to form opinions about things and people, and if we do that we keep our opinions to ourselves, so as to control the damage that can be done by our wrong judgment. Remember the *end* can come even while we are judging someone else and acting on that judgment.

KILL

"Thou shalt not kill." Exodus 20:13

Kill is defined as 'to deprive of life, cause the death of.' Whether we actually kill someone or cause the death of someone, we are guilty of killing that person. King David did not actually kill Uriah, but by his instruction he was responsible for causing Uriah's death. God pronounced judgment upon David and the child, which was born, as a result of David's sin, was afflicted and died. The commander of the battle could have ignored the king's instruction and so spare Uriah's life, and probably face the consequences. Some individuals commit murder and are able to afford very skilled lawyers, who get them off the charges. Some persons hire hit men/women to kill a spouse or an enemy, and face the consequences if discovered. Some females, who have unwanted pregnancies, have the babies killed by abortion. Some even die during or after the abortions. All who have survived abortions should repent of the act. But the most important thing should be to examine the reasons for the abortion, and if it was due to fornication or adultery, to repent of that act also that resulted in the unwanted pregnancy, and ask for God's help not to sin, a sin that can lead to the desire to have an abortion. Let us be aware that the *end* can come while we are in the very act of killing someone.

MENPLEASERS

In Ephesians 6: 5-6 we read "Servants, be obedient to them that are your masters according to the flesh, with fear and trembling, in singleness of your heart, as unto Christ; not with eyeservice, as menpleasers, but as the servants of Christ, doing the will of God from the heart."

Sometimes we act in a particular way when our pastor, our brethren or our supervisors are around, and we show our true selves when we think no one is looking. However, lest we continue in that way and feel comfortable, let us know that even when mankind is not watching, God is watching at all times, and He is the One who matters. He knows when we cover up something which we should have done better. He knows when we do things contrary to employers' policy, as soon as they turn their backs. Some employees have been disciplined for using agency's funds/items, in ways that they were not approved to do. Some have done that very act and have not been discovered and feel very comfortable about it, basking in their 'luck'.

God has given mankind the knowledge to make cameras, which can be hidden and record acts without persons knowing. Some of these very recordings have been used to catch criminals, such as individuals who ill- treat children or the elderly, whom they are paid to look after. How much more will God discover our sinful acts; *"For the eyes of the Lord run to and fro throughout the whole earth, to show himself strong in the behalf of them whose heart is perfect towards him."* 2 Chronicles 16:9. Let us ask God to help us to refrain from doing anything, that is not pleasing to Him; for while we are indulging in such behavior, or have indulged and not repented, our *end* can come and our fate will be sealed with the devil in hell.

MURMUR

> *1 Corinthians 10:10 "Neither murmur ye, as some of them also murmured, and were destroyed of the destroyer."*

The dictionary defines murmur as 'a mumbled or private expression of discontent; to complain in a low tone on in private.' In Numbers 14 the children of Israel murmured against God and their leaders and incurred God's wrath, and were punished. Sometimes we feel that we have to complain about everything, although such actions do not change the situation. Sometimes we make the situation worse when we complain to others, and the complaint is misrepresented to someone else. Sometimes there is either reprisal, for we feel betrayed when we find out that, what we said was shared with someone else. Sometimes God may provide a spouse for us who does his/her best to please us. However we compare them with others and may murmur over the cost of our birthday gifts, our anniversary gifts, our valentine gifts or our Christmas gifts. Some husbands murmur over their wives' cooking, the care of the house, her lack of energy at the end of a hard day or even her physical appearance. God commands us not to murmur: so let us obey his words, so that it would be well with us and with our Souls if our *end* comes suddenly.

OFFEND

> Matthew 18:6 states "But whoso shall offend one of these little ones which believe in me, it were better for him that a millstone were hanged about his neck, and that he were drowned in the depth of the sea."

The dictionary defines offend as 'to irritate, annoy or anger, to cause resentful displeasure in, insult, to harm or cause pain.' We have seen how offending God's children, is taken very seriously by Him. Let us therefore strive not to offend anyone. Luke 17:1 states "It is impossible but that offenses will come: but woe unto him, through whom they come." Sometimes we feel it is our privilege to tell persons off in the most offensive manner, especially when we have an audience. Let us remember that, while we are impressing the crowd, with our offensive behavior, we are sealing our fate if, our *end* comes before we can repent. The way to ensure our place with God, in heaven, is guaranteed is to do the things that are pleasing in His sight. We may say that the scripture refers to children. Let us take note that we are all children in the sight of God, because He is our Father.

PERVERSENESS

> Proverbs 15:4 "A wholesome tongue is a tree of life: but perverseness therein is a breach in the Spirit."

The dictionary defines perverse as 'willfully determined not to do what is expected or deserved, contrary; characterized by, or proceeding from such a determination; wayward or cantankerous, wicked or corrupt.' Let us ask God to help us not to be perverse in or words or actions. God's Word tells us what we are to do in relation to Him, and in relation to our fellow human beings. Sometimes we feel we have the right to be nasty towards others. Sometimes we justify our actions by saying, that those individuals whom we hurt are not doing the right things. If that were the case, and if we cannot correct the individuals in love, take the situation to God in prayer. He knows all the facts; and what we may consider to be the situation may not even be the case. So while we may assume wrongly or rightly and act accordingly we may be preventing ourselves from spending Eternity with God, if we do not repent before our *end* comes.

POLLUTE

> *Ezekiel 20:31 states "For when ye offer your gifts, when ye make your sons to pass through the fire, ye pollute yourselves with all your idols, even unto this day: and shall I be enquired of you, O house of Israel? As I live, saith the Lord God, I will not be inquired of by you."*

Pollute is defined as 'to make foul or unclean, to make impure or morally unclean, defile'. When our lives become polluted our relationship with God is broken. It must be noted that we demonstrate how polluted we are by what comes out of our mouth. *In Mark 7:20- 23 we read: "That which cometh out of a man, that defileth the man. For from within, out of the heart of men, proceed evil thoughts, adulteries, fornication, murders, thefts, covetousness, wickedness,, deceit, lasciviousness,, an evil eye, blasphemy, pride, foolishness: All these evil things come from within, and defile the man."* We may not eat flesh and may not wear certain types of garments, but if what comes out of us is offensive we are in spiritual trouble. We have to repent, and thank God for grace. Once restored, we must ask God to help us not to sin again.

PRATING

> *Proverbs 10.8 states "The wise in heart will receive commandments: but a prating fool shall fall."*

The word prating comes from the root word prate, which means 'to talk excessively and pointlessly, babble; to utter in empty or foolish talk' We must remember that God hears every word we speak; hence we must ask him to fill our mouths with words of wisdom and encouragement. Sometimes it is better if we do not speak instead of speaking idle words. *Matthew 12:36 states "But I say unto you, that every idle word that men shall speak, they shall give account thereof in the day of judgment."* Sometimes we talk a lot and even offend/hurt others with what we say, and, when we are confronted we say we are joking. Let us ask God to help us to so speak, that our words will not close the gate of heaven to us if our *end* were to come while we are speaking.

RASH

> *Ecclesiastes 5:2 advises "Be not rash with thy mouth, and let not thine heart be hasty to utter anything before God: for God is in heaven, and thou upon the earth: therefore let thy words be few."*

Rash is defined as 'acting hastily or without due consideration.' Sometimes when we are in situations we make promises, even to God. Sometimes when we are angry we say things that we regret afterwards. Some advise us to count to 10 when we are angry, before we respond/react to a situation. However only help from God can keep us from making rash statements. Therefore let us seek help from God, especially when we are getting angry, lest we speak or act in a manner that will cause not to be bound for heaven if our *end* comes while we are speaking.

REFRAIN

> *1 Peter 3:10 states "For he that will love life, and see good days, let him refrain his tongue from evil and his lips that they speak no guile."*

Refrain, according to the Webster Dictionary is 'to keep oneself from doing or saying something.' We have to ask God, with the help of the Holy Spirit to help us to refrain from doing/saying anything that offends man and/or God. Sometimes we assume that words are just words, and they do not hurt as physical wounds would hurt. However, words sometimes hurt more than physical wounds do; as we can attend to a physical wound until it is healed; but the emotional wounds cannot be seen and touched and some people are so broken by our words that they do irrational things. Let us ask God to help us to speak uplifting words at all times, or if we cannot let us refrain from speaking, so that God would be pleased with us.

REFUSE

*"And the Lord said unto Moses, How long refuse ye to keep
my commandments and my laws" Exodus 16:28.*

The Webster dictionary states that refuse means 'to decline, and
implies non acceptance of something. It is direct and emphatic expressing
a determination not to accept what is offered or proposed'. This statement
was uttered after the children of Israel refused to adhere on how to
collect the manna, which God provided for them. We have been offered
redemption from our sins through the Blood of Jesus. We have accepted
Jesus' forgiveness and have become a part of the family of God. We are
now required to live according to God's Word which dictates how we
should live, in order to please God and be able to spend eternity with
Him when our *end* comes.

REND

*Joel 2:13 states "And rend your heart, and not your garments, and turn
unto the Lord your God: for He is gracious and merciful, slow to anger, and of
great kindness, and repenteth him of the evil."* Rend is defined as 'to distress
the heart with painful feelings; to tear one garments out of grief or rage.'
Let us show deep remorse when the Holy Spirit convicts us, that we have
sinned against God, who is merciful, as *Psalm 51:17 states "a broken and
a contrite heart, O God, thou wilt not despise."* If we are convicted by the
Holy Spirit, or told by someone, that we have offended an individual,
regardless of their status, and we are going to apologize; let us do it from
a sincere heart, knowing that the One who holds the keys to heaven sees
the heart, while man only hears our words. It is the heart that has to
experience the sorrow for what we have done. In ancient times men tore
their garments and sat in ashes, to show that they were sorry for their
sins. God does not want a public showing with an unrepentant heart.
He wants our hearts to be sorrowful.

RENDER

> 1 Thessalonians 5:15 states "See that non render evil for evil unto any man, but ever follow that which is good, both among yourselves, and to all men." 1 Peter 3:9 states "Not rendering evil for evil, or railing for railing: but contrariwise blessing; knowing that ye are there unto called, that ye should inherit a blessing."

'To give in return' is how the dictionary defines render. If we are going to believe the promises in the Bible we can afford not to render evil for evil for our God has said *"Vengeance is mine, I will repay." Romans 12:19.* Sometimes we feel that our merciful God will not do justice to our enemies, so we try to avenge ourselves. It is understandable to feel very angry towards individuals, who have greatly violated us. Sometimes our actions get us into serious trouble and then we turn to God for help, despite the fact that we were disobedient to his Word. Let us strive to be obedient to God's word. Let us ask Him for grace to be obedient to Him, as we do not know when the *end* will come.

REPENT

> ." Luke 13:3 says "I tell you, nay, but except ye repent, ye shall all likewise perish." Acts 3:19 states "Repent ye therefore, and be converted, that your sins may be blotted out, when the times of refreshing shall come from the presence of the Lord."

Repent is defined as 'to be penitent for one's sins and seek to change one's life for the better'. Repent is so profound a word in the Christian's life that I must dwell on it a while. We must repent for ourselves. Repentance is something from the heart. In order for repentance to occur one must feel very sorry in the heart, for what one has done. Sometimes we tell people with our mouths, that we are sorry for something we have done. We assume that, that is what they want to hear. We then go and do the same thing over and over again. Often this is how an abusive spouse behaves. The same thing happens with our relationship with God. We say we are sorry for the sins we have committed; whether it is lying, stealing, etc. Then we continue to do the same thing. Living in fornication is one of the sins we repent of and sometimes continue to do. However, man may not know if we really mean what we are saying, when we say it, as man does not see our hearts, God knows for He sees our hearts and He knows our thoughts afar off. Let us realize that when we are truly sorry for our sins, we will turn from our wicked ways. We must, however, acknowledge that we cannot do it in our own strength, and we must ask God to help us and He will us, because He is *"not willing that any should perish, but that all should come to repentance."* 2 Peter 3:9

SEPARATE.

> *"Wherefore come out from among them, and be ye separate, saith the Lord, and touch not the unclean thing; and I will receive you."* 2 Corinthians 6:17.

Separate is defined as to 'keep apart, divide, disconnect, disassociate, become parted from a mass or compound, take or go in a different direction.' As we give our lives to God and we sanctify ourselves for His service, we may have to separate ourselves from some of our old acquaintances. This would be necessary because some of the things we used to do, we would have to refrain from doing them any longer. The word of God says *"let him that stole steal no more."* Ephesians 4:28. In like manner all of the other sins we used to commit, we would have to stop committing them. Some of our acquaintances may not respect our decision, so we would have to choose whom we would serve/please. Committing sin, whether by our words or our actions, would have to become a thing of the past, as *1John 3:9 states "Whosoever is born of God doth not commit sin."* When God called Abraham he had to leave family and acquaintances and go where God led him. Abraham obeyed God and we see God made and kept several promises to him. Let us now look at individuals in our lives, who would cause us to indulge in acts, which would separate us from God, and separate ourselves from those individuals, if they cannot respect our decisions, to live our lives pleasing to God, so that we would be able to enter heaven, when our *end* comes, and spend Eternity with God.

VOW

Deuteronomy 23:21 states "When thou shalt vow a vow
unto the Lord thy God, thou shalt not slack to pay it: for the
Lord thy God will surely require it of thee; and it would be
sin in thee." Verse 23 states: "That which is gone out of thy
lips thou shalt keep and perform; even a free will offering,
according as thou has vowed unto the Lord thy God, which
thou hast promised with thy mouth."

The dictionary defines vow as 'a solemn promise, pledge or personal commitment; a solemn promise made to a deity or saint, committing oneself to an act, service or condition; to pledge or resolve solemnly to do'. Sometimes when we are in a serious predicament we bargain with God and tell Him that if He resolves the situation, in our favor, we would serve Him faithfully. God comes true for us and we immediately forget that we made that vow. Our Bible records a man who meant what he vowed. Judges 11:30-39 states "And Jephthah vowed a vow unto the Lord, and said, If thou shalt without fail deliver the children of Ammon into mine hands, then it shall be, that whatsoever cometh forth of the doors of my house to meet me, when I return in peace from the children of Ammon, shall surely be the Lord's, and I will offer it up for a burnt offering..... And Jephthah came to Mizpeh unto his house, and behold, his daughter came out to meet him with timbrels and with dances: and she was his only child; beside her he had neither son nor daughter. And it came to pass when he saw her, that he rent his clothes, and said, I have opened my mouth unto the Lord, and I cannot go back..... And it came to pass at the end of two months, that she returned unto her father, who did with her according to his vow which he had vowed."

While we associate vowing with God, it is also to be taken seriously when we make a vow/pledge to our fellow human beings. Sometimes we make promises to others, and we take it lightly and do not keep them. Sometimes we vow, knowing right there and then, that we have no intention of keeping that vow. 'Do this for me and I will pay you that. Lend me some money and I will repay it as soon as I get my pay, taxes etc.' Sometimes in order to convince someone, who may appear hesitant to our vow, we even get to swearing to make our point. While sometimes we may genuinely forget to pay what we had promised, we would not get angry if we were given a kind reminder. However we put our Souls in a balance when we deliberately break our vows. When we became saved, we promised that we would walk with God the rest of our lives. Let us keep that vow, so that we would spend Eternity in heaven when our *end* comes.

Bridget Cordis

Conclusion

Tomorrow is promised to no man. As a matter of fact the next second is not guaranteed to anyone. The young, the adolescent, the matured, the old and the very old cannot predict their next minute. When we plan a trip we are all familiar with ETD (estimated time of departure) and ETA (estimated time of arrival). Sometimes those timings do not occur as planned, and in worse case situations those arrivals never happen. Ships sink, planes crash, vehicles collide. Bad weather, and all sorts of unforeseen circumstances can cause well thought out plans not to materialize.

Sometimes individuals leave home telling their loved ones they would be back shortly, or by the usual time (from church, school or work). Shootings in the church, school or workplace leave those promises unfilled. Robbery by a passenger/customer, being involved in an accident, freak or otherwise, can cause those promises to remain unfulfilled. The fire fighter who leaves home, and then has to rush into a burning building, may have a heart attack and never return home. The policeman who answers that domestic violence call, may find that he/she is attached and killed and never returns home.

Many persons leave their homes with a genuine promise that they would be back and never did.

Then there are situations, when individuals promised to see their loved ones upon their return. Some never saw them alive again; as they may have perished in a fire, become a victim of a home invasion or succumbed to carbon monoxide poisoning. Some might have also met their *end* at the hand of a jealous lover, or ex-lover, angry relative, or might have taken their own lives.

Regardless of how their lives ended, whatever spiritual state they were in at that time would determine where they would spend Eternity. The same goes for each and every one of us.

As Christians fall prey to those sins that so easily beset us, some of us rely on the scripture that says "*My little children, these things write I unto you, that ye sin not. And if any man sin, we have an advocate with the Father, Jesus Christ the righteous.*" 1 John 2:1 The Webster dictionary defines an advocate as 'a person who speaks or writes in support of a cause, person etc; a person, who pleads for or in behalf of another, intercessor; a person who pleads the cause of another in a court of law.' In the court of law someone has to give the advocate the facts (whether true or fabricated) so that the advocate can make the pleas before the judge.

When Christians sin we have to approach our Advocate, Jesus and tell Him of our sin(s) and our regret, so that He can present it to the Father. If our *end* comes, and meets us in our sinful state before we are able to speak to our Advocate, (through prayer), our hope of entering into heaven is vanished, as we can tell our Advocate nothing.

Some claim that *once saved; always saved.* When we become saved our names are recorded in the Lamb's book of life. When the disciples were excited that the devils were subject unto them they were told in *Luke 10:20 "Notwithstanding in this rejoice not that the spirits are subject unto; but rather rejoice because your names are written heaven".* However, not because the names are recorded in heaven means it is a permanent situation. This is how Revelation 3:5 says our names will remain in the Book of life: "*He that overcometh, the same shall be clothed in white raiment; and I will not blot out his name out of the book of life, but I will confess his name before my Father, and before his angels".* By reason it shows that our names can be blotted out if we do not overcome the sins of this world.

The unbeliever may ask 'How do you know that heaven is where you may be when your end comes'? When our Lord and Savior, Jesus was leaving, He said "*In my Father's house are many mansions: if it were no so, I would have told you. I go to prepare a place for you. And if I go and prepare a place for you, I will come again, and receive you unto myself; that where I am, there ye may be also." John14: 2-3.* Jesus is in heaven as Stephen when he was being martyred said "*Behold, I see the heavens opened, and the Son of man standing on the right hand of God." Acts7:56.* That is where we will be with Jesus, our Lord and Savior if our *end* finds us living a life pleasing in the sight of God.

Thank God for our blessed hope. It is worth all the sacrifices we have to make in order to spend Eternity with Jesus. *"For the Lord himself shall descend from heaven with a shout, with the voice of the archangel, and with the trump of God: and the dead in Christ shall rise first: then we which are alive and remain shall be caught up together with them in the clouds, to meet the Lord in the air: and so shall we ever be with the Lord"*. 1 Thessalonians 4:16-17.

Glory Hallelujah!!!